Cycling for Nutrition 102

Fast Weight Loss

By Cathy Wilson

Copyright © 2013

Income Disclaimer

This book contains business strategies, marketing methods and other business advice that, regardless of my own results and experience, may not produce the same results (or any results) for you. I make absolutely no guarantee, expressed or implied, that by following the advice below you will make any money or improve current profits, as there are several factors and variables that come into play regarding any given business.

Primarily, results will depend on the nature of the product or business model, the conditions of the marketplace, the experience of the individual, and situations and elements that are beyond your control.

As with any business endeavor, you assume all risk related to investment and money based on your own discretion and at your own potential expense.

Liability Disclaimer

By reading this book, you assume all risks associated with using the advice given below, with a full understanding that you, solely, are responsible for anything that may occur as a result of putting this information into action in any way, and regardless of your interpretation of the advice.

You further agree that our company cannot be held responsible in any way for the success or failure of your business as a result of the information presented in this book. It is your responsibility to conduct your own due diligence regarding the safe and successful operation of your business if you intend to apply any of our information in any way to your business operations.

Terms of Use

You are given a non-transferable, "personal use" license to this book. You cannot distribute it or share it with other individuals.

Also, there are no resale rights or private label rights granted when purchasing this book. In other words, it's for your own personal use only.

Cycling for Nutrition 102

Fast Weight Loss

By Cathy Wilson

Table of Contents

Introduction

Cycling Nutrition 102 for Fast Weight Loss is a dynamic book that describes the importance of fueling your mind and body "right" for fast and long lasting weight loss. Cycling for weight loss is a fun and effective route to get slim, healthy and happy quickly.

This book integrates scientific backed strategies to help teach you how to eat healthy to:

* Energize your body for cycling
* Strengthen your lean muscle
* Lose fat
* Sharpen your mind
* Improve work productivity
* Stabilize relationships

We will discuss . . .
- Factors in Healthy Eating
- Macronutrients and Micronutrients

- Tips and Tricks to Improve Eating Habits and Get Physically Fit
- Benefits of Cycling
- Nutrition and the Effects on Your Mental
- Weight Loss and Cycling Fitness

Most importantly we will be discussing a PLAN OF ACTION that will turn your world upside down, from tired and grumpy to energetic, thin and alive!

This book digs beneath the surface to understand the basics of what nutrients your body needs, when, how much and why. You will see just how easy and effective these weight loss concepts are. Add cycling to this and you are killing two birds with one stone. You will be accelerating your fat loss, boosting mood, strengthening your mental, deterring disease, ridding your body of deadly toxins and triggering your brain to release endorphins naturally that will leave you feeling like you're on cloud nine.

You are in charge of you and with an open mind and commitment to "better" your health one step at a time. There's no result except to succeed. This book will take your hand and show you the way and if you learn just one new positive piece of information to help you better yourself mind, body and soul, then my mission is complete!

It's time for you to open your mind and look for some positive to apply!

Nutrition Your Body Needs

Nutrition is simply the food and drink intake your body needs and the various chemical and physiological processes triggered to break down and transport the nutrients to locations to be used. Good nutrition will enable your body to have all the energy requirements necessary to maintain good health and optimal system output.

You are what you eat is so very true. If you choose to eat processed high fat foods loaded with sugary calories and very little nutrition, you will increase the likelihood of becoming obese, lethargic, ill from disease, depressed, overly anxious, side lined from injury and you'll be less satisfied with life in general. Studies back up the fact that unhealthy people tend to see their glass as half empty always.

How come good nutrition is critical?

Various nutrients are essential in keeping your body and mind strong. They help to repair damaged cells and bodi-

11

ly tissues, maintain the health of bones and internal systems, ensure plenty of energy is available and you are warm and comfortable.

Optimal health requires great nutrition long term which also helps deter serious disease from sneaking in as a result of toxic build up and ruining your day and your life. Most illnesses and disease that devastate are preventable if better nutrition is practiced. In fact, medical scientists believe up to thirty percent of all cancers and a large percentage of heart disease is directly related or triggered because of poor eating and nutrition. That's got to shock you into reality here!

Good nutrition is achieved by taking a few steps back and paying attention to your body, filling it full of protective and antioxidant rich fruits and veggies, protein sources, complex carbohydrates that help with longer term energy and toxic waste remove with adequate fiber, milk products and sources providing calcium, good fats to provide energy and keep your mind sharp and all the critical vitamins and minerals your body needs to keep your energetic and alive. Ready to stand up to the challenges daily life gives you and fight off those nasty free radicals looking to manifest disease? The choice is all yours.

Of course 6-8 glasses of water each day is great to start with. Your body can technically last up to a week without food, but just 2-3 days without water. Water hydrates your body, increases energy and enables your internal systems to function with fluidity.

In order to stand strong against the test of time your body needs . . .

* Protein

* Fat
* Carbohydrates
* Vitamins and Minerals
* Water

The amount of food you need each day is dependent on your age, genetics, body composition, height and weight, activity level, health status, stress level, sleep patterns and other lifestyle factors. Each individual is unique, as are your specific nutritional needs. Regular eating is important so your body has a "ready to use" supply of nutrients when required. This will help to stabilize blood sugars, deterring diseases like diabetes and help you to level moods and energy, in other words, skipping your afternoon lows and ensuring more constant and quality energy during the day.

Each "kind" of food you eat or nutrient you eat is absorbed and utilized differently, each for a specific purpose.

Your body is made to move and everything you do requires energy. From walking to smiling, running and even sleeping all use calories and energy. Proper nutrition is going to help you help yourself make the most of life.

What are calories?

Your nutrition is made of calories. Each food you eat has calories and this means in order for your body and mind to function optimally you need to eat calories.

A calorie is basically one unit of energy. When referring to nutrition a calorie is the energy measurement in the food you are eating. A small banana has approximately 80 calories of energy and 5 minutes at a moderate pace on the treadmill burns about 50 calories of energy. I hope this makes sense.

The fact is anything that has energy has calories. We just tend to use it when referring to food and exercise. It's a measurement tool we use to ensure we are giving our body what it needs to reach a certain result. For instance, in general if you eat less calories than your body needs and exercise more, you should lose weight. It's a numbers game which your body burns calories to start.

Why do you need calories?

Nutrition gives your body calories or energy you need to live. Without calories your organs wouldn't work, cells would die and you would be no more. As humans we get our nutrition or calories in the form of food and drink.

How many calories does your body need?

Of course it would be too easy to have a standard answer here. Even two people that are exactly the same weight and height can have different nutritional requirements and hence need a different number of calories to maintain their current weight.

If you are looking to lose weight, one fairly precise place to start is to figure out your BMI or Body Mass Intake to calculate the approximate number of calories your body needs each day. From here you can determine what amounts of what foods you require to maintain or lose weight.

To lose weight, you would set out a plan where you were eating healthier foods in smaller quantities, less calories and fat overall, combined with exercise like cycling and weight training to boost your metabolism and burn energy faster.

You can either use an online BMI calendar or have you nutrition expert calculate it for you using your:

* Sex
* Age
* Weight
* Height
* Activity Level

Plugging these factors into the equation will give you your BMI

Normal healthy BMI range is between 18.5 and 24.9 and this translates to a weight range that applies to your height, age and other factors specifically. If you are under 18.5 in general you are considered underweight. Over 24.9 is considered extremely obese and means you need to take immediate action.

Keep in mind this is just a starting place from which to measure and there are exceptions to the rules where a person may be under 18.5 percent and be quite healthy. Body Fat Caliper testing is much more accurate.

The most accurate results can be done by specific individual physiological testing. The more accurate you are here, the more precise you can be when looking to what you should be eating and how much.

My Thoughts . . .
It is important to know what nutrition your body needs if so you can adjust it to meet your health and wellness goals. If you want to lose weight you're going to want to sensibly decrease the number of calories consumed,

lower your unhealthy fat intake and increase your essential vitamins and minerals. Be careful not to dip too low with the calories because if you aren't getting enough energy to sustain the proper function of your internal systems, your body will start to shut down. It will go into emergency mode and try to store fat and reserve energy. Even if you are just eating carrot sticks your body will slow your metabolism and try and store every calorie as fat for later use.

Why?

Simply because your body can't trust you to feed it the vitamins and minerals it needs to keep you healthy and it truly doesn't know when you are going to feed it again. Sad, but true.

Bottom line is you've got to feed your body to encourage it to boost your metabolism and burn more fat and calories. Finding the balance is a trial and error process essential in reaching your weight loss goals of looking and feeling fabulous!

Macronutrients - Micronutrients and You

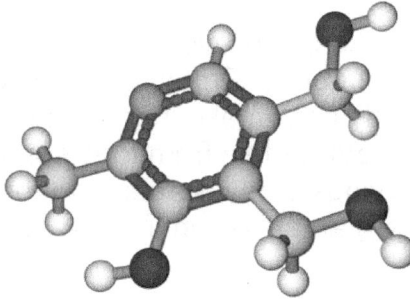

Let's start first with macronutrients which are essential nutrition your body needs in larger doses. The three macronutrients are:

Protein
Carbohydrates
Fat

Proteins are basically larger molecules that are made up of amino acids which your body and cells need to function optimally. Protein is required to:

* help form strong body structures
* assist with fluid body function
* help regulate all the cells of your body
* ensure the correct formation and upkeep of tissues and organs and other body parts including skin, hair, muscles and bones

Did you know that protein makes up about TWENTY percent of your body weight?

Another function of proteins is to work as carrying agents to take oxygen through the circulatory system via blood (hemoglobin). You may also know proteins as enzymes, hormones and antibodies.

To make this picture crystal clear, protein is a part of every single cell in your body. Protein is an essential nutrient because your body can't make it or store it. This means you need to get your protein from food sources each day. Two or three servings a day is adequate for most normal function. If you are an athlete in training you might need a little more.

Protein sources can be either complete or incomplete.

Complete Protein is usually from animal sources or meat. Beef, turkey, chicken or fish are examples that have all 20 different amino acids present, making them complete and easily absorbed. Quinoa is a plant based protein that is an exception to the rule as it's considered a complete protein.

If you don't eat meat, you can get your "complete" protein by combining various plant sources.

Incomplete Protein are protein sources, usually plant based that don't have all the amino acids on their own so you need to mix and match or combine them to get your protein.

So you might mix beans with cottage cheese or have some nut butter on whole grain bread. Lentils, tofu, soy milk and tempeh are also good sources of protein. A wide variety of foods each day will help you ensure you give your body the protein it requires to shine.

If you don't give your body enough protein, it will look to break down the protein or muscle you have already worked hard to build to use for energy. It seems to defeat the purpose of working out hard to build your body strong!

Here are the 20 different amino acids in protein:

* Alanine, arginine, asparagines, asparic acid
* Cysteine
* Glutamic acid, glutamine, glycine
* Histidine
* Isoleucine
* Leucine, lysine
* Methionine
* Phenylalanine, proline
* Serine
* Threonine, tryptophan, tyrosine
* Valine

I think that's twenty! Luckily this is an "introductory" book just in case!

Each of these 20 amino acids can be mixed and match in a zillion different ways to make a protein, specifically for functions of the body. These AA are organic molecules which are derived of hydrogen and carbon, oxygen, nitrogen and on occasion sulphur.

A gram of protein is the same as a gram of carbohydrate and has 4 calories. Is your brain hurting yet?

Serving Sizes:
- a deck of cards for lean meat

- 3/4 cup of veggies
- 2x2 inch cube of cheese
- 1 cup skim milk
- 1/2 cup yogurt or cottage cheese
- 3/4 cup beans, lentils

This gives you a nice starting point anyway because most people are prone to heart attacks when they learn are distorted their belief of a serving size is.

Carbohydrates are typically found in pasta, cereal, bread and the majority of cakes, pastries and sweets. They have a reputation for causing fat gain but this is misguided for a couple reasons. First, anything in excess can cause fat gain. Secondly, there are different kinds of carbs and a simple carbohydrate in excess is much more likely to cause weight gain.

The Science of It . . .

Carbohydrates are organic compounds which have sugars or saccharide. This food is used by your body to create glucose which is used for energy. In specific, it's an enzyme in your body called amylase that breaks carbohydrates apart to make glucose which give you energy. Glucose can be used for immediate energy or your body can save it for a rainy day.

Let's have a gander at the two different types of carbohydrates:

Simple Carbs

This kind of carbohydrates is simple and broken down quickly to be used by your system. Sugars naturally found in fruit and vegetables are simple or foods such as processed candy and sweets have it. The difference between these simple sugars is the natural sugars found in fruits for example, contain essential vitamins and minerals your body needs to be healthy. The processed sugars in packaged foods do not have healthy vitamins and minerals your body requires for optimal function. This means they are waste of your eating and in excess they WILL make you unhealthy and FAT!

Here are a few common simple sugars you will find on labels:

* corn syrup
* dextrose
* brown sugar
* maltose
* molasses
* malt syrup

Be VERY careful when purchasing packaged foods because manufacturers often try and hide the gynormous amounts of sugar with disguised names you might not recognize.

Complex Carbohydrates

These are the carbs your body and mind need to function like a well oiled machine. Fiber and starches are ones you might recognize and because of their more complex nature they take time to be broken down for use. Examples of complex carbs are:

* peas, corn, potatoes and other vegetables
* lentils and beans
* bread, pasta, rice and crackers
* oatmeal
Your body needs about 5-6 servings to start of good carbs. Whole grain bread, brown rice and pasta, sweet

potato and steamed veggies are excellent choices to give your body the complex carbohydrates it requires to help you burn calories, gain energy for the long run and blast fat. Fiber and essential vitamins and minerals are in these carbs and this is why choosing "brown" over white in this department makes you as wise as an owl.

Sample Serving Sizes:

- 1 slice of whole grain bread or 1/2 whole wheat bagel
- 1 small sweet potato
- 1 small banana
- 1 orange or 1/2 grapefruit
- 1 cup spinach or 3/4 cup carrots
- 1 cup soy milk

Diversity is critical here and making sure you are balancing out the healthy carbohydrates you are getting. As you can see, eating is a science and finding the right "fit" for you is going to take some time. Some foods might be easily absorbed by your body better than others and you need to work with your body to figure out how to build your body lean and strong for the long run. This starts with understanding what your body needs and why.

What are the Benefits of Carbohydrates?

* Carbohydrates help prevent your body for using muscles for fuel.
* The fiber found in complex carbohydrates will help regulate your internal systems and purge harmful toxins from your body naturally.
* Having fiber in your digestive tract will help slow the digestive process and regulate blood sugar levels.
* Specific carbs help with digestion because they give nutrients to produce good bacteria in the gut.

* They can also increase the amount of calcium that's absorbed into your body.

Carbohydrates are essential in helping your body drop fat and get healthy. They also help to make you feel fuller longer and push you towards eating less.

Fat is a macronutrient that is essential to your existence. Unfortunately, we live in a society that understands and recognizes only the negatives of fat and not the good. In other words, fat gets a bad rap and we need to take the time to understand it and take the time to use it "right."

What is Fat?

It's a nutrient critical for life. It helps supply your body with energy and helps other essential nutrients do what they're supposed to in order to keep you strong and healthy.

Fat is normally soluble in water and chemically it's recognized as "triesters" of glycerol in combination with fatty acids. At room temperature, they may be either liquid or solid. Most healthy or unsaturated fats are liquid at room temperature. Unhealthy or saturated fats like butter are in solid form. A "lipid" is any sort of fat.

Fat Meaning Just to Keep Things Straight

Fats - Any kind of fat. Although most of the time this refers to fat that's solid at room temperature.

Oils - These are fats that that are liquid at room temperature, don't mix with water and feel greasy to the touch.

Lipids - Just think of this as a universal fat term encompassing fats in solid or liquid form.

Humans and animals require fat to survive. Our societal problem is we get too much fat accumulation and obesity is the dire consequence. Experts report that regular exercise can genetically influence how your body stores and uses fat. This is a light at the end of the tunnel for many.

Examples of Animal Fats

* Real cream, lard, creamy butter, fat on meat
Examples of Vegetable Fats
* Peanut oil, safflower oil, almond oil, vegetable oil, olive oil

The two main types of fat are:

Unsaturated or "Good" Fat

If you put your science hat on, this type of fat has fat molecules that aren't saturated with atoms of hydrogen. Every molecule is structured so just one hydrogen molecule is attached. The verdict is mono or unsaturated fat sits on the fence. It's not good or bad for you, but studies show it may reduce the risk for development heart disease, which is a very good thing.

Saturated, Trans Fat or "Bad" Fat

This fat is loaded with hydrogen atoms and experts unanimously agree saturated fat in large amounts over a longer period of time will increase your risk for developing numerous serious diseases including heart disease, Alzheimer's and diabetes.

Eating this fat will increase blood lipids, which interferes with internal system and will likely eventually trigger stroke and cardiovascular disease.

24

These fats are found in meat product, chicken or turkey skin, milk and various milk products and in processed foods like cakes, cookies, pastries and other sweet treats.

Note - An exception to the rule here is coconut oil. It is considered a saturated fat, but has enormous benefits from healing skin issues and helping with digestion to improving energy and strengthening hair.

Trans Fat - These are VERY dangerous fats. In fact, they are processed fats that have been genetically modified to have a longer shelf life and more stability. These fats are not required for survival and science proves they only interfere with good health. Fast food restaurants and commercial food industry uses these toxic fats. They are so dangerous that many cities of the world are trying to ban the use of trans fats.

What amount of fat do you need?

Although babies and growing children need a little more, adults over the age of 20 need about 25-30% daily fat intake. The majority of fat should be healthy unsaturated. The bottom line is most of us need to reduce our total fat consumption to get healthy and lose weight. By learning new healthy eating habits and increasing daily physical activity, including both muscle building and cardiovascular exercise like cycling, you will set your body and mind up to lose weight fast and for good.

Micronutrients

In simple terms micronutrients are essential for your survival. They are needed in small doses for various physiological functions. In humans they are needed in trace amounts of less than 100 mg each day. These in-

25

clude: iron, chromium, cobalt, copper, iodine, zinc, selenium, manganese and molybdenum.

As well, vitamins are micronutrients, organic and necessary in small doses.

13 vitamins required are:

- A, C, D, E, K
- Thiamine, riboflavin, niacin, pantothenic acid, biotin, vitamin B-12, folate
Eating a healthy well-balanced diet should give you all the vitamins and minerals you need to stay strong and healthy. It's also normal for your body to produce vitamin D and K. If you are vegan, B12 may be lacking.

NOTE: If you are lacking in specific vitamins and minerals you may develop certain diseases.

My Thoughts . . .
This is where it's important to open your mind to the big picture and learn as much as you can about what nutrients you body needs and why. The better you understand the function of your internal and what each nutrient does to benefit your mental and physical, the better decisions you can make to melt fat quickly, permanently, boost your energy, battle off disease, strengthen your muscles and skeletal system and build your mind and body super strong.

I could write a book just about micro and macronutrients there's so much to learn and perhaps I will. Now that you have the basics of what your body needs intrinsically, let's move on.

Cycling and Eating

You might think that because you are cycling or exercising you can eat anything you want. In general, you likely have a little more freedom with your calories because you are working your body hard but if you are aiming to slim down and lose weight, it's important you pay attention to what foods you are eating and how much.

It's vital you give your body enough lean protein and healthy carbs to boost your metabolism, build lean muscle, blast fat and give your mind and body the energy it requires to perform and feel fabulous.

Cyclists in training need to consume:
* low-fat, high carb food choices that give lasting energy
* plenty of fluids for hydration with water as the best option
* lean protein, particularly before and after training
* healthy fat in small amounts

"Good" carbohydrates are what your body needs. 5-6 servings per day should suffice unless training rigorously. Great examples include:
- fresh fruits and vegetables
- beans, sweet potato and legumes
- whole grain bread, rice and pasta

If you happen to be cycling more than an hour, you should refuel with some extra carbs to keep your energy stores up. For the most part though, unless you are training intensely for more than 90 minutes, plenty of cool, refreshing water is all your body needs. The nutritional replenishment comes shortly after you've trained. Replacing the energy stores you have used up with a healthy snack consisting of both lean protein and "good" carbohydrates is important.

Long after you've finished cycling your internal bodily systems are still burning energy and in order to maximize the burn and increase your weight lost, energy in the form of useable fuel needs to be readily available. This restorative energy is also required for energy repair and building, both of which happen after the fact when exercising.

Did you know that your body continues to burn fat and calories at a heightened rate up to an hour AFTER you've finished exercising? That's even more incentive to get your heart pumping and circulatory system moving, muscles working hard and adrenaline hopping. Regular cycling or any exercise for that matter is good for you both physically and mentally.

My Thoughts . . .
Cycling and eating go hand in hand, particularly if you're looking to blast fat fast, get lean and toned, boost energy

levels, decrease the risk for serious disease and become for productive in work and life.

Whenever you are eating with the focus of losing weight, it's important to pay attention to the food choices you are making. Extra energy is required when training hard with cycling, but not as much as you might think. Make sure you are always getting plenty of water to keep your body hydrated, mind and body functioning optimally. It's also important to have a lean protein and good carbohydrate snack of about 300 calories about 60-90 minutes before training, then again shortly after.

If you want your body to increase its metabolic rate to burn more energy, build lean muscle, get rid of fat and keep it off for good, then you need to feed it with smarts. Sounds great to me, how about you?

Tips to Improve Eating Habits

It doesn't matter who you are or what lifestyle you live. There are always things you can be doing to better your health when it comes to eating. It's not about being perfect, but rather about keeping your eyes peeled for practical and "doable" eating changes you can make that will stick for the long run. Trial and error works best here because let's face it, there are some things you just don't want to give up. That's perfectly okay. You deserve to eat healthy, be happy and have control and contentment with the food choices you are making.

So where do you start when aiming to "better" your comfortable eating habits?

First things first, you need to get your head on straight and I don't mean literally here. It's important that you actually WANT to make changes in your eating. There is a huge difference with regards to long-term success between "thinking" and "wanting" here.

You MUST commit to stick with the changes you are making if you are going to reach your weight loss and health and wellness goals. Otherwise, you'll just ride the roller coaster of what I call "ping-pong" health forever, meaning you make healthy eating choices that don't quite become habit or your new normal. This means you will systematically fall right back into your comfortable, yet unhealthy eating habits of days past and wallow in self misery. Sad, but true. We all do it from time to time and when you mentally decide to stop fooling around and get determined to stick with your NEW, HEALTHIER and FAT FIGHTING eating habits you WILL reap the rewards fast!

So now that you've committed, here are a few pointers to help you make your fat-loss dreams a reality. Tidbits of information you can take a gander at and use what adheres to YOUR preferences and tolerances. In other words, the tips that catch your attention and you can honestly see working for you. I'm not going to say this very often, but right now it's all about you.

* Eat Breakfast!

Most of us are either breakfast eaters or we're not. What I have to tell you here is that studies show people that eat a healthy breakfast regularly are leaner, more fit, have less disease and live longer and more satisfying lives than people that don't. SCIENCE says to do it so I think you better!

This also makes sense because after your long winters nap your system is depleted of nutrients. You are running on empty and your body physiologically needs energy in the form of healthy food choices, not to mention the importance of your mental here because if you aren't thinking and feeling great about yourself because you're starving hungry and just plain ornery, how can you expect to be happily productive?

Eat a healthy breakfast EVERYDAY and you won't have anything to worry about!

* Keep A Food Journal

As tedious as this sounds, it works! Often we need a wakeup call when it comes to the food we eat and in what amounts. A food journal is a great way to force yourself to acknowledge and digest the amount of food you are eating each day.

Often this "shocker" is enough to trigger change or at least the "thought" of change, which is where it all starts. By recording every single morsel of food you eat each day, you are making yourself accountable for your actions. Do you really want to be eating 6 pancakes for breakfast each day with butter and syrup, two "Pop tarts," a glass of sugared juice and a pastry or two? Not likely. Problem is we create eating habits that aren't based on intrinsic hunger, but on emotion or maybe just plain learned habit.

Chances are you aren't even aware of all the food you are eating and don't even know why. A food journal will force you to stand up to the plate and recognize your unhealthy actions. Digging to the route of the problem where you can choose to take action or not, the choice is yours to make.

* Avoid Deprivation

Food experts agree one of the surefire ways to set yourself up for failure is to feel deprived when it comes to food. Wouldn't you agree? As humans I hesitate to say we "want, want, want" and then want a little more. We simply don't like not having in all areas of life, not just eating.

We get used to the foods we enjoy and if they happen to be taken away for ANY reason we'll cry, well not exactly, but you know what I mean. Healthy eating is all about enjoying the foods you're eating AND moderation. It's a give and take relationship that most of us have grossly distorted over time, transforming it into an unhealthy "all or nothing" scenario that leaves us fat and unhealthy, battling gynormously depressing physical and mental issues WE have created all on our own.

This is an introductory book so I won't get into the consequences of our actions in detail, but I'm certain you get what I'm talking about here.

We've learned the unhealthy habit of eating the whole bag of cookies all the time instead of enjoying "guilt-free" just one or two on occasion. It's got to be the whole family size bag of chips in one sitting instead of enjoying a handful and if still hungry grabbing an able or pear.

Our society has learned how to take the "treats" of the world which would normally be harmless in the big picture and distort them so enormously they end up transforming into a mountain of trouble for our health. Mentally and physically a piece of chocolate cake shouldn't cause issue. It becomes an issue for most because we don't have perspective or control to "moderate" the treats in life we should allow ourselves on occasion. So what's the solution?

Learn to allow yourself a special few unhealthy foods in small amounts and sparingly without feeling guilty or deprived. You can have your cake and eat it too, but this will take time and patience to learn how to do it so it doesn't backfire on your weight loss plan.

* Pay Attention

By chewing slowly and paying attention to the food you are eating you'll eat less and less weight. What you're trying to learn, is how to pay attention to the delicious flavorful foods you are eating and knowing when to stop.

You DON'T need to eat until you pop. How about stopping before you are full, wait 15 or 20 minutes and eat a little more if your tummy is saying you're still hungry. Physiologically it takes at least this much time for your stomach to rely the message to your noggin that you are full, satiety and ready to stop eating.

If you are mindlessly eating in front of the television, it's pretty much a guarantee that you will run right through the stop sign telling you that you're full. We all know how awful it feels when we've eaten too much and just feel disgusted with ourselves.

Slow down and smell the flowers when you are eating and this awareness alone should help you curb your appetite, fuel your system for the "right" reasons and drop poundage in the process.

* Baby Steps First

It's important that you don't overdo it here with too much change. Overwhelming yourself and being unable to keep up with your personal expectations makes it pretty impossible to succeed in establishing healthy eating habits that work for you.

One step at a time considering your preferences and tolerances is how it's got to be. If you've never been a breakfast person before don't start off with a full breakfast right after rolling out of bed. Give yourself some time to adjust and start off trying to eat a piece of fruit or maybe a slice of whole grain toast with peanut butter before heading out the door.

Slowly, but surely your mind and body will adjust and you can add a little more nutrients to your morning eating ritual when the time is right.

If you are used to eating fast food for dinner every day don't cut it out cold turkey. To start cut it down to having it just 3-4 times a week and eating healthy homemade meals the other nights. Slowly, but surely you will work your way up and in time, with patience and perseverance you will remove most of the fast food eating and crave the healthy food choices.

Perspective and belief is important. You might not believe this will ever happen because you are sitting on this side of the fence. When you get to the other side you WILL make it happen and understand why and that you are too important not to put your best food forward here.

* Water First

Water is not only something your body needs to survive, to keep you thinking clearly, run your bodily system efficiently and provide energy. Water will also give you that "full" feeling that helps you consciously recognize just how hungry you are.

Getting into the habit of having a glass of water BEFORE you decide to eat will help you eat less. Studies show this is both a mental signal to your brain to pay attention to eating and also reassurance to yourself that you aren't always hungry when you think you are. Often water will do the trick and maybe a little bit of food. It should not be a truckload of food and no water.

Most definitely drinking water is a smart move. It ensures you are fully hydrated and naturally decreasing the amount of food you eat is bonus.

* Pay Attention to Portions

Unfortunately, society today is always expanding portion sizes and along with it the waistlines of Americans. Restaurant portions are the worst because for the most part they are at least 2-3 times larger than the average person needs.

We get used to this and when we eat at home instead of having 3/4 of a cup of pasta like we should, we habitually teach ourselves to expect two or three cups. Anything less leaves us feeling like we just got the short end of the stick.

Experts agree that just by adjusting serving sizes to what they should be, the weight loss in total for the population would be astronomical. Most would be eating 2-3 times less food and this would mean smaller pants for all.
To start people need to understand portion sizes and adhere this with healthier wholesome eating choices. It's a win-win for everyone.

Meat Portion - about the size of a deck of cards
Beans - approximately 3/4 cup
Fresh Vegetables - one cup
Fresh Fruits - one piece or 3/4 - 1 cup
Breads - one slice or half a bagel
Cereals - 3/4 - 1 cup

Eggs - 1
Milk - 1 cup
Yogurt - 3/4 cup
Cheese - 2x2 inch cube (just think how many servings are on a piece of pizza!)
Salad Dressing or Oil - 1-2 tablespoons
Peanut Butter - 1 tablespoon
Pasta or Rice - 3/4-1 cup
Nuts - 1/4 cup
Raisins - 1/2 cup

By no means is this a complete list, but it's a good start to help you understand and accept the reality with regards to serving size. You've got to start somewhere right?

My Thoughts . . .
These are just a few pointers to help you establish improved eating strategies that will last a lifetime. This isn't about going through the motions of change and hopping right back on that roly-poly roller coaster of weight change. If that's what you want, then you're wasting your time with this book.

If you are looking to make positive eating changes and are willing to do what it takes to make them stick, then you WILL succeed and gain from this book. You truly are important and I'd like to see you put these tips to good use!

Nutrition and Your Mental

So what has your nutritional choices got to do with your mental perception and function? The simple answer to this is EVERYTHING. Your mental and physical are dependent on one another. What affects one WILL affect the other and by paying attention to the food choices you are making you are going to help ensure your head's on straight and you're headed in the right direction to reach your personal weight loss goals and so much more. Hope this sounds fabulous to you?

Yes your mental health is reflective of genetics, your environment and age, but it's also sensitive to the nutrition you give your body on a daily basis. The fats, proteins, carbohydrates and vitamins and minerals you choose to fill your body up with directly affect your mental capacity. Scientists believe the food you eat plays a critical role in the prevention of serious disease, the progression and qualified management of mental issues inclusive of depression, anxiety, Alzheimer's, ADHD and even schizophrenia. The connection here has been estab-

lished and researchers are driving full speed ahead un-
covering the specifics so we have better information from
which to act.

It's long since been understood the food choices you
make are reflective of your physical appearance and your
emotional stability throughout life. It starts from pre-
conception and continues until we die.

Just look at the benefits breastfed babies have over bottle fed infants in terms of brain function. Studies show
optimal brain function in breastfed babies over bottle fed
and that's just the surface, a starting point. It's because of
the presence of natural essential fatty acids in the milk
these infants are in the pole position.

Also proven is the increased cognitive capacity in children that start their day with a wholesome breakfast.
Along with this, kids that eat high-fat processed foods for
the most part tend to be fatter, have more behavioral issues and health problems than children who eat
healthier. Those are the straight facts.

A Little Bit of Science . . .

Your brain consists of billions of nerve cells that enable
your brain to effectively communicate with all parts of
your bodily systems. Most of your brain is made up of fat
which of course is directly reflective of your nutrition
choices. Amino acids are the building blocks of protein
and these AA are involved in the communication of the
brain. Various other neurotransmitters are also involved
and each determines how well your brain can communicate.

This is where your eating habits come into place. Choosing to fuel your body with unhealthy processed high-fat

foods will cause interference in the function of your brain. Over time this can trigger disease, increase stress and be stamped "trouble" for you, your thinking and physical function.

Good foods like fresh berries for example are brain friendly. They are rich with antioxidants that help protect your brain and keep your body disease-free. Fact is how you eat directly affects your brain.

By ensuring your diet is full of lean protein, complex carbohydrates, essential fats, water, vitamins and minerals, you are making the right move toward losing weight and getting our body healthy and strong for good.

My Thinking . . .
This of course, is the basics of the importance of health eating and strong mental function. It's not just about losing weight and getting happy with your physical. Your mental is just as important if not more here.

Choosing to pay attention to how your fuel your body is only going to increase your overall mental capacity, giving it the vital nutrients it requires to transmit information to all parts of your body and enable optimal function of your body, supportive of good health. As always it's your choice. Do yourself a favor and "think" about it.

Benefits of Cycling

Cycling is a fabulous way to get your body into great shape. It can help you gain energy, lose fat, build lean solid muscle, think clearer and minimize the conscious attention you have for annoying aches and pains.

Exercise has so many health benefits from increasing optimism, zapping fat and lowering blood pressure, to increasing mobility to and motility to improving circulation. The sky is the limit and to each his or her own here. That said, here are a few tried, tested and true cycling benefits!

* Lowers Cholesterol
* Decreases Risk of Cancer
* Increases Energy
* Improves Cardiovascular Function
* Betters Mood
* Stabilizes Blood Sugar
* Improves Sleep Quality
* Strengthens Skeletal System

* Decreases Risk of Injury
* Increases Lean Muscle
* Increase Metabolism
* Helps Initiate Weight Loss
* Contributes to Weight Stabilization
* Lowers Diabetes and Heart Disease Risk
* Increase Life Expectancy
* Decreases Resting Heart Rate
* Lowers Fat or Lipids in Blood
* Improves You Psychosomatically
* Betters Recovery Time from Illness, Disease and Injury

Cycling is fantastic because you can safely do it at any age. Whether you are 4 or 85, you can hop on a bike and get your heart rate pumping to benefit your health, physically and mentally.

By cycling, you are also challenging your heart more than you would just by walking and there is less stress on your joints and muscles. This means less risk of injury and a whole lot less wear and tear.

Cycling is also something you can do just about anywhere. It's versatile, practical, social, and fun. It can be productive if you use it as a method of transportation to get to or from work. Just think about how friendly you are being to the environment if you can commute to work on your bike!

The Risks?

There are risks with anything in life. It comes to perspective, common sense and safety. Experts agree the benefits of cycling outweigh the risks more than 20 to 1. It is important to run this by your health provider before commencing just in case. Always better to be safe than sorry!

My Thoughts . . .
Cycling is exercising that can be personalized to suit your needs. If you're looking to lose weight fast, it can be done in the form of intense interval training to force your body to work harder and more effectively to lose fat. It also can be used to get some exercise in on those days when you just aren't feeling so hot. Just try to understand that it's always better to do something rather than nothing, at least for the most part or unless a doctor has instructed otherwise.

Where there's a will there's a way and using cycling to help get your body lean, fit and healthy is one smart move!

Myths Debunked

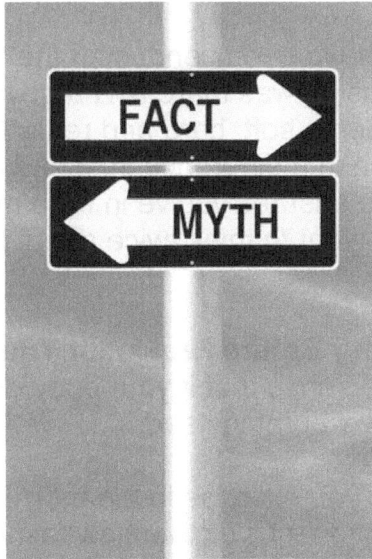

There always seems to be a spoiler in the bunch, wouldn't you agree? Rather than focus on that, we are going to shed some positive light on some of those cycling fibs out there. With accurate and practical information you be able to take the shortcut to your goals.

Myth - Less Fit People Perspire More. Many people believe the less fit you are or the more fat you have, the sweatier you'll get faster, that exercising is going to make you sweat buckets more-so than a fit person

Truth -.With more cycling experience you body will learn to get better at cooling, it will actually sweat earlier to keep your body temperature down. Most people that are physically fit will sweat faster and often in larger quantities than a person not so dedicated to regular exercise.

Myth - Harder Tires Are Better. You would think that a harder bicycle tire allows you to cycle faster.

Truth - Studies have been conducted that prove otherwise. The conclusion was there isn't a physiological difference between a soft, hard and really hard tire. It's not enough to make a difference in speed anyway. In fact, a harder tire ensures you've in for a much bumpier ride so you may want to think twice about how hard you pump yours.

Myth - By Cycling Before Breakfast You'll Burn More Fat. It may make sense that if your body doesn't have food in it fat will be burnt instead.

Truth - Whether you exercise in the morning, on an empty stomach or not doesn't dictate how fast or how much fat you burn. Nutrition experts report it's the total number of calories you take in each day, how much your exercise, age, body composition and lifestyle factors that for the most part dictate your fat loss. Also take note that studies show most heart attacks and strokes occur in the morning with cyclists.

Myth - Shaving Makes Faster. Many believe shaving your legs when cycling helps you become aerodynamically faster.

Truth - This one just isn't scientifically backed. Muscles may look better when shaved, gravel may wash out easier from scrapes when hairless, but nothing more. Swimming however is another matter altogether and if you need a lawnmower to make your legs smooth you might want to seriously consider it!

My Thoughts . . .
There are facts and fibs with just about everything in life and cycling in no exception. Change is tough enough in life and starting with the truth will just help you get happy with cycling sooner. Sounds good to me!

Sample Eating Plan for Cycling

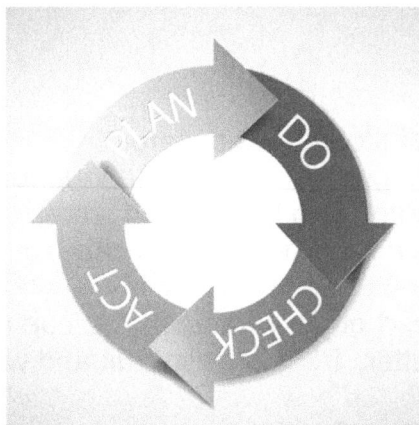

What you eat prior to and after your cycling is critical for optimal performance and effective calorie burning. One major source of fuel for your muscles are carbohydrates that are simple stored or packed away in your muscles prior to exercising in the form of glycogen, which is readily available energy.

Topping up glycogen stores takes some time and this means if you aren't eating properly and filling up your stores your performance or the amount of time you are able to cycling will suffer. This is more critical for cyclists in training but important to know regardless.

What to Eat Before Exercise . . .

Glucose is what your body wants to use for energy. The best thing you can do before cycling is to fuel your body with easily digestible carbohydrates, choosing whole grain pastas, rice, cereals and fruits.

In general people that eat fairly healthy generally have enough glycogen stored for about 90 minutes of hard exercise. Drinking 2-3 cups of water is also important. Your muscles, mind and body need to be hydrated fully for proper function.

Sample snacks . . .

- banana, handful of nuts and water
- piece of whole grain bread with peanut butter and water
- 3/4 oatmeal with fresh berries and water
- 1/2 whole grain bagel with cream cheese, an apple and water
- fruit smoothie -1 cup low-fat milk, 1/2 cup low-fat yogurt, tbsp peanut butter, 1/3 cup fresh fruit and water

What to Eat After Cycling . . .

Now that you've finished training it's important to eat to restore your depleted nutrient stores. The experts agree the ratio should be about 4:1, with 4 grams of carbs for every gram of protein. This will ensure your body gets its energy stores refilled and there's enough protein for continued muscle growth and increased metabolic rate, meaning you'll burn fat and calories longer.

Sample snacks . . .

- whole grain oatmeal with skim milk and water
- 1/2 whole grain bagel with egg and water
- low-fat yogurt with fresh berries and water
- chocolate milk and almonds

In a pinch, an energy bar will do the trick. It's important to pay attention to the carbohydrates, protein, sugar and fat though.

In general, when cycling or training up to an hour per day you'll want to add at least one extra serving of carbohydrates and protein, with plenty of water. Pay attention to your body, how you are feeling, energy levels and don't be afraid to adjust your eating. When aiming to lose weight you need to do a little experimenting because you want to give your body enough energy to burn fat and calories but not more than your body needs or you won't be successful in dropping weight.

Sample Day of Eating With Moderate Cycling

We are going to assume for food calculation purposes you are moderately active with cycling, are 5 feet 2 inches tall and 140 pounds. Your calorie intake to maintain your weight is approximately 2,000 calories per day and your aim is weight loss.

Breakfast
Poached egg with whole grain toast
3/4 cup low-fat yogurt with 1/2 cup fresh berries
Water

Exercise
40 minutes moderate cycling, 15 minutes weights

Snack
Banana and 1/4 cup nuts, cheese string
Water

Lunch
2 cups spinach, grilled chicken breast, fresh veggies, drizzle salad dressing
1 cup fresh fruit
Water

Snack

Handful of dried fruit
Hardboiled egg
Water

Dinner
Grilled salmon
2 cups mixed vegetables
Baked sweet potato
Water

Keep in mind this is just to give you an idea of the foods you should be eating. Adjust as you see fit according to preferences and tolerances. Pay attention to your bodily signals. You may need to eat a little more or less to reach your weight loss goals. Use this template to get you started on the right foot!

My Thinking . . .
Now you have a solid idea of what your body needs to perform. You are at the starting gates and have the ammunition to make it to YOUR finish line. Don't bolt out of the starting gates and take care to take it one step at a time so you can make your new changes stick. If you really want to make the changes to lose weight and get fit you can. This information you have gathered will get you started. Now it's time for you to get serious and start building!

Advantages of Cycling to Lose Weight

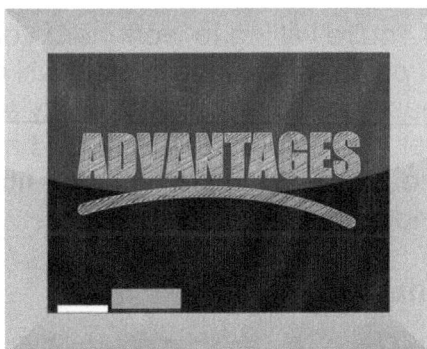

There are lots of different fast and effective ways to lose weight and cycling is just one of them. Cycling is something that just about anyone can do, it's fun and effective at getting your heart rate up and muscles working hard to burn fat and calories.

Here are a few clear advantages to cycling to lose weight.

* Little Skill Required

Cycling is exercise you probably learned as a child and never forgot, just like walking. You don't have to take classes or any structured course to learn how to bike. Chances are pretty good you can just hop on and go!

* Practical

Cycling is excellent because you can do it just about anywhere. You can even fit it into your routine as a method of getting to work or going to grab groceries. When exercising has more than one purpose, it tends to stick.

* Great Calorie Burning

With cycling, if you're willing to work hard you can burn a heck of a lot of calories. Intense cycling will challenge muscles, increase cardiovascular capacity and burn up to 700 calories per hour! Both anaerobic and aerobic conditioning can take place which pushes your fitness level to the extreme and zaps fat FAST.

* Easy on Joints

Lots of exercise is very hard on muscles and joints. Something that gets noticed more as we age. Cycling is advantageous because has less stress on your joints than say walking or running. This means there is less chance of injury and if you're already dealing with a chronic injury with hips or back, biking is something you can safely do.

Pretty much anyone in any condition can do at least some biking and benefit their overall good health too.

* Work at Your Own Pace

Cycling is excellent in that you can work at your own pace. If you want to progress faster towards better fitness and faster weight loss then you pedal harder. You are in complete control of your progress and that's awesome!

* Fun and Effective

One of the best features of cycling is that it's fun and effective. You can go for an intense ride through the park enjoying the scenery while burning fat. How about getting a group of friends together to go for a bike up the mountain or along the trails? If you enjoy cycling there will always be a challenge out there if you want it.

My Thoughts . . .
Cycling is an excellent route to get your body and mind in shape while losing weight and having fun. Take it one step at a time making sure you consider your personal goals, preferences and tolerances are important for success. You are in the driver's seat here and it's time to stop thinking about it and just start peddling. The harder you peddle the faster you're going to get there!

One of the best features of cycling is that it's a social feature. You can go for an intense ride through a park enjoying the scenery while burning fat. It's about getting a group of friends together to go on a hike up the route ... or go along for a ride. If you enjoy exercise then there will always be a challenge out there if you want it.

My Thoughts...

Cycling is an excellent route to use if you want to get in shape while losing weight and having fun. Have a look step at a time working sure you consider your metabolism, your performance and every aspect are improving the more ... it. You are the driver's seat more so do it the way you want it and ...

58

Final Thoughts

You are in charge of you and if you aren't happy with your weight, body shape or life it's YOU that has to decide to change. Excuses will get you nowhere. We all lead busy lives and you have to make the changes and stick with them if you want your pants to start falling off you!

Understanding how your body works is critical in getting the results you want for your efforts. Learning to fuel your body effectively with healthy food choices with proper servings is only going to push you faster toward your weight loss goals.

Losing weight is going to give you energy, fight off disease, release positive vibes, increase metabolism, reduce aches and pains, improve mobility and motility, make chronic conditions more manageable and flip your life switch to optimistic. This will open doors of opportunity you never realized existed. How exciting is that?

If you learned just one piece of useful information from this book them I've succeeded in helping you better yourself!

It's time for you to take what you've learned and put it into serious action. You deserve the best in life and with an open and willing mind you will get it. Looking great and feeling fantastic are just bonus!

We have the choice to look for the positive or the negative in life. You can choose to lift someone up or to stomp on them. Writing is my passion and I work hard at it, with the goal of helping make people better. If you gain a new piece of knowledge, read something that makes you think, or perhaps even smile a few times, then I am happy and content!

Life's just too short not to tune into optimism. If your glass is half full, then I invite you to read my writing, and if you have a minute to spare when you're through, **I would appreciate your review.** This will help me better myself and my writing. I thank you in advance and appreciate you.

CPSIA information can be obtained at www.ICGtesting.com
Printed in the USA
LVOW01s1513150514

385952LV00019B/1039/P